MY PET
BETTA FISH LOGBOOK

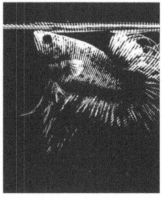

THIS BOOK BELONGS TO:

MY PET
BETTA FISH LOGBOOK

ALL ABOUT YOUR FISH

PHOTO/DRAWING

NICKNAME:

DOB:

SPECIES:

SEX:

COLOR & MARKING:

LINCENSE #:

ADOPTION PLACE:

MORPH:

MICROCHIP:

HOW WE MET:

HOW HE/HER GOT NAME:

OWNER'S INFORMATION

NAME:

ADDRESS:

PHONE: EMAIL:

VET INFORMATION

CLINIC: VET:

ADDRESS:

PHONE: EMAIL:

IMPORTANT NUMBERS

NAME:	PHONE:	ADDRESS:

NOTES:

MEDICATION RECORD/VET VISITS

DATE:	REASON FOR VISIT:	NEXT VISIT:
DATE:	REASON FOR VISIT:	NEXT VISIT:
DATE:	REASON FOR VISIT:	NEXT VISIT:
DATE:	REASON FOR VISIT:	NEXT VISIT:
DATE:	REASON FOR VISIT:	NEXT VISIT:
DATE:	REASON FOR VISIT:	NEXT VISIT:
DATE:	REASON FOR VISIT:	NEXT VISIT:

MEDICATION

MEDICATION:	DATE:	NOTES:

EXPENSES

DATE:	SOURCE	DESCRIPTION:	AMOUNT:

EXPENSES

DATE:	SOURCE	DESCRIPTION:	AMOUNT:

ABOUT BETTA FISH

Life span

- 3-5 years with proper care

Size

- 2 1/2 inches long, not including tail

Diet

- Carnivore

Minimum Aquarium Size

- 1 gallon or larger

Routine care checklist guide

Daily Activity

 Feed 2-4 pellets, 1 to 2 times daily.

 Remove uneaten food

 Check filter

 Check water temperature

 Check other equipment (if used)

 Look for odd behavior & signs of illness or fin damage.

Weekly Activity

 Test check water quality once a week

 Change 1/3 water 2 x week

 Vacuum up uneaten food and waste.

 Check pH and bacteria levels.

Monthly Activity

 Check filters, replacing media as necessary.

 Clean fake plants, decorations, and algae.

 Vacuum up all waste and uneaten food from gravel.

 Check water quality and pH levels.

MY PET
BETTA FISH LOGBOOK

DAILY CHECKLIST

Activity	WEEK OF						
	SUN	MON	TUE	WED	THU	FRI	SAT
Feed 2-4 pellets, 1 to 2 times daily.	☐	☐	☐	☐	☐	☐	☐
Remove uneaten food	☐	☐	☐	☐	☐	☐	☐
Check filter	☐	☐	☐	☐	☐	☐	☐
Check water temperature	☐	☐	☐	☐	☐	☐	☐
Check other equipment (if used)	☐	☐	☐	☐	☐	☐	☐
Look for odd behavior & signs of illness or fin damage.	☐	☐	☐	☐	☐	☐	☐

NOTES:

WEEKLY, MONTHLY CHECKLIST

WEEKLY ACTIVITY   DATE:

- [ ] Test check water quality once a week
- [ ] Change 1/3 water 2 x week
- [ ] Vacuum up uneaten food and waste.
- [ ] Check pH and bacteria levels.

MONTHLY ACTIVITY   MONTH:

- [ ] Check filters, replacing media as necessary
- [ ] Clean fake plants, decorations, & algae
- [ ] Vacuum up all waste & uneaten food from gravel
- [ ] Check water quality & pH levels

HEALTH CHECKLIST   DATE:

- [Y] [N] Active and alert
- [Y] [N] Eats regularly
- [Y] [N] Vibrant colors
- [Y] [N] Undamaged fins
- [Y] [N] Reacts aggressively to outside stimulus

NOTES:

DAILY CHECKLIST

	Activity	WEEK OF

		SUN	MON	TUE	WED	THU	FRI	SAT
	Feed 2-4 pellets, 1 to 2 times daily.	☐	☐	☐	☐	☐	☐	☐
	Remove uneaten food	☐	☐	☐	☐	☐	☐	☐
	Check filter	☐	☐	☐	☐	☐	☐	☐
	Check water temperature	☐	☐	☐	☐	☐	☐	☐
	Check other equipment (if used)	☐	☐	☐	☐	☐	☐	☐
	Look for odd behavior & signs of illness or fin damage.	☐	☐	☐	☐	☐	☐	☐

NOTES:

WEEKLY, MONTHLY CHECKLIST

WEEKLY ACTIVITY   DATE:

- [ ] Test check water quality once a week
- [ ] Change 1/3 water 2 x week
- [ ] Vacuum up uneaten food and waste.
- [ ] Check pH and bacteria levels.

MONTHLY ACTIVITY   MONTH:

- [ ] Check filters, replacing media as necessary
- [ ] Clean fake plants, decorations, & algae
- [ ] Vacuum up all waste & uneaten food from gravel
- [ ] Check water quality & pH levels

HEALTH CHECKLIST   DATE:

- Y / N Active and alert
- Y / N Eats regularly
- Y / N Vibrant colors
- Y / N Undamaged fins
- Y / N Reacts aggressively to outside stimulus

NOTES:

DAILY CHECKLIST

Activity	WEEK OF						
	SUN	MON	TUE	WED	THU	FRI	SAT
Feed 2-4 pellets, 1 to 2 times daily.	☐	☐	☐	☐	☐	☐	☐
Remove uneaten food	☐	☐	☐	☐	☐	☐	☐
Check filter	☐	☐	☐	☐	☐	☐	☐
Check water temperature	☐	☐	☐	☐	☐	☐	☐
Check other equipment (if used)	☐	☐	☐	☐	☐	☐	☐
Look for odd behavior & signs of illness or fin damage.	☐	☐	☐	☐	☐	☐	☐

NOTES:

WEEKLY, MONTHLY CHECKLIST

WEEKLY ACTIVITY   DATE:

- [ ] Test check water quality once a week
- [ ] Change 1/3 water 2 x week
- [ ] Vacuum up uneaten food and waste.
- [ ] Check pH and bacteria levels.

MONTHLY ACTIVITY   MONTH:

- [ ] Check filters, replacing media as necessary
- [ ] Clean fake plants, decorations, & algae
- [ ] Vacuum up all waste & uneaten food from gravel
- [ ] Check water quality & pH levels

HEALTH CHECKLIST   DATE:

- [Y] [N] Active and alert
- [Y] [N] Eats regularly
- [Y] [N] Vibrant colors
- [Y] [N] Undamaged fins
- [Y] [N] Reacts aggressively to outside stimulus

NOTES:

DAILY CHECKLIST

Activity	WEEK OF						
	SUN	MON	TUE	WED	THU	FRI	SAT
Feed 2-4 pellets, 1 to 2 times daily.	☐	☐	☐	☐	☐	☐	☐
Remove uneaten food	☐	☐	☐	☐	☐	☐	☐
Check filter	☐	☐	☐	☐	☐	☐	☐
Check water temperature	☐	☐	☐	☐	☐	☐	☐
Check other equipment (if used)	☐	☐	☐	☐	☐	☐	☐
Look for odd behavior & signs of illness or fin damage.	☐	☐	☐	☐	☐	☐	☐

NOTES:

WEEKLY, MONTHLY CHECKLIST

WEEKLY ACTIVITY   DATE:

- [ ] Test check water quality once a week
- [ ] Change 1/3 water 2 x week
- [ ] Vacuum up uneaten food and waste.
- [ ] Check pH and bacteria levels.

MONTHLY ACTIVITY   MONTH:

- [ ] Check filters, replacing media as necessary
- [ ] Clean fake plants, decorations, & algae
- [ ] Vacuum up all waste & uneaten food from gravel
- [ ] Check water quality & pH levels

HEALTH CHECKLIST   DATE:

- [Y] [N] Active and alert
- [Y] [N] Eats regularly
- [Y] [N] Vibrant colors
- [Y] [N] Undamaged fins
- [Y] [N] Reacts aggressively to outside stimulus

NOTES:

DAILY CHECKLIST

📅 Activity	WEEK OF _____
	SUN MON TUE WED THU FRI SAT

Activity	SUN	MON	TUE	WED	THU	FRI	SAT
Feed 2-4 pellets, 1 to 2 times daily.	☐	☐	☐	☐	☐	☐	☐
Remove uneaten food	☐	☐	☐	☐	☐	☐	☐
Check filter	☐	☐	☐	☐	☐	☐	☐
Check water temperature	☐	☐	☐	☐	☐	☐	☐
Check other equipment (if used)	☐	☐	☐	☐	☐	☐	☐
Look for odd behavior & signs of illness or fin damage.	☐	☐	☐	☐	☐	☐	☐

NOTES:

WEEKLY, MONTHLY CHECKLIST

WEEKLY ACTIVITY   DATE: [   ]

- [ ] Test check water quality once a week
- [ ] Change 1/3 water 2 x week
- [ ] Vacuum up uneaten food and waste.
- [ ] Check pH and bacteria levels.

MONTHLY ACTIVITY   MONTH: [   ]

- [ ] Check filters, replacing media as necessary
- [ ] Clean fake plants, decorations, & algae
- [ ] Vacuum up all waste & uneaten food from gravel
- [ ] Check water quality & pH levels

HEALTH CHECKLIST   DATE: [   ]

- Y N Active and alert
- Y N Eats regularly
- Y N Vibrant colors
- Y N Undamaged fins
- Y N Reacts aggressively to outside stimulus

NOTES:

DAILY CHECKLIST

Activity	WEEK OF						
	SUN	MON	TUE	WED	THU	FRI	SAT
Feed 2-4 pellets, 1 to 2 times daily.	☐	☐	☐	☐	☐	☐	☐
Remove uneaten food	☐	☐	☐	☐	☐	☐	☐
Check filter	☐	☐	☐	☐	☐	☐	☐
Check water temperature	☐	☐	☐	☐	☐	☐	☐
Check other equipment (if used)	☐	☐	☐	☐	☐	☐	☐
Look for odd behavior & signs of illness or fin damage.	☐	☐	☐	☐	☐	☐	☐

NOTES:

WEEKLY, MONTHLY CHECKLIST

WEEKLY ACTIVITY   DATE: _____

- [ ] Test check water quality once a week
- [ ] Change 1/3 water 2 x week
- [ ] Vacuum up uneaten food and waste.
- [ ] Check pH and bacteria levels.

MONTHLY ACTIVITY   MONTH:

- [ ] Check filters, replacing media as necessary
- [ ] Clean fake plants, decorations, & algae
- [ ] Vacuum up all waste & uneaten food from gravel
- [ ] Check water quality & pH levels

HEALTH CHECKLIST   DATE: _____

- Y N Active and alert
- Y N Eats regularly
- Y N Vibrant colors
- Y N Undamaged fins
- Y N Reacts aggressively to outside stimulus

NOTES:

DAILY CHECKLIST

Activity	WEEK OF
	SUN MON TUE WED THU FRI SAT

	Activity	SUN	MON	TUE	WED	THU	FRI	SAT
	Feed 2-4 pellets, 1 to 2 times daily.	☐	☐	☐	☐	☐	☐	☐
	Remove uneaten food	☐	☐	☐	☐	☐	☐	☐
	Check filter	☐	☐	☐	☐	☐	☐	☐
	Check water temperature	☐	☐	☐	☐	☐	☐	☐
	Check other equipment (if used)	☐	☐	☐	☐	☐	☐	☐
	Look for odd behavior & signs of illness or fin damage.	☐	☐	☐	☐	☐	☐	☐

NOTES:

WEEKLY, MONTHLY CHECKLIST

WEEKLY ACTIVITY　DATE:

- [ ] Test check water quality once a week
- [ ] Change 1/3 water 2 x week
- [ ] Vacuum up uneaten food and waste.
- [ ] Check pH and bacteria levels.

MONTHLY ACTIVITY　MONTH:

- [ ] Check filters, replacing media as necessary
- [ ] Clean fake plants, decorations, & algae
- [ ] Vacuum up all waste & uneaten food from gravel
- [ ] Check water quality & pH levels

HEALTH CHECKLIST　DATE:

- [Y] [N] Active and alert
- [Y] [N] Eats regularly
- [Y] [N] Vibrant colors
- [Y] [N] Undamaged fins
- [Y] [N] Reacts aggressively to outside stimulus

NOTES:

DAILY CHECKLIST

Activity	WEEK OF

| | SUN MON TUE WED THU FRI SAT |

Feed 2-4 pellets, 1 to 2 times daily. ☐ ☐ ☐ ☐ ☐ ☐ ☐

Remove uneaten food ☐ ☐ ☐ ☐ ☐ ☐ ☐

Check filter ☐ ☐ ☐ ☐ ☐ ☐ ☐

Check water temperature ☐ ☐ ☐ ☐ ☐ ☐ ☐

Check other equipment (if used) ☐ ☐ ☐ ☐ ☐ ☐ ☐

Look for odd behavior & signs of illness or fin damage. ☐ ☐ ☐ ☐ ☐ ☐ ☐

NOTES:

WEEKLY, MONTHLY CHECKLIST

WEEKLY ACTIVITY   DATE:

- [ ] Test check water quality once a week
- [ ] Change 1/3 water 2 x week
- [ ] Vacuum up uneaten food and waste.
- [ ] Check pH and bacteria levels.

MONTHLY ACTIVITY   MONTH:

- [ ] Check filters, replacing media as necessary
- [ ] Clean fake plants, decorations, & algae
- [ ] Vacuum up all waste & uneaten food from gravel
- [ ] Check water quality & pH levels

HEALTH CHECKLIST   DATE:

- Y / N Active and alert
- Y / N Eats regularly
- Y / N Vibrant colors
- Y / N Undamaged fins
- Y / N Reacts aggressively to outside stimulus

NOTES:

DAILY CHECKLIST

📅 Activity	WEEK OF

		SUN	MON	TUE	WED	THU	FRI	SAT
🪱	Feed 2-4 pellets, 1 to 2 times daily.	☐	☐	☐	☐	☐	☐	☐
⊗	Remove uneaten food	☐	☐	☐	☐	☐	☐	☐
	Check filter	☐	☐	☐	☐	☐	☐	☐
🌡	Check water temperature	☐	☐	☐	☐	☐	☐	☐
🔧	Check other equipment (if used)	☐	☐	☐	☐	☐	☐	☐
🔍	Look for odd behavior & signs of illness or fin damage.	☐	☐	☐	☐	☐	☐	☐

NOTES:

WEEKLY, MONTHLY CHECKLIST

- [ ] Test check water quality once a week
- [ ] Change 1/3 water 2 x week
- [ ] Vacuum up uneaten food and waste.
- [ ] Check pH and bacteria levels.

MONTHLY ACTIVITY   MONTH:

- [ ] Check filters, replacing media as necessary
- [ ] Clean fake plants, decorations, & algae
- [ ] Vacuum up all waste & uneaten food from gravel
- [ ] Check water quality & pH levels

HEALTH CHECKLIST   DATE:

- Y / N Active and alert
- Y / N Eats regularly
- Y / N Vibrant colors
- Y / N Undamaged fins
- Y / N Reacts aggressively to outside stimulus

NOTES:

DAILY CHECKLIST

📅 Activity	WEEK OF _____
	SUN MON TUE WED THU FRI SAT

		SUN	MON	TUE	WED	THU	FRI	SAT
🐛	Feed 2-4 pellets, 1 to 2 times daily.	☐	☐	☐	☐	☐	☐	☐
⊗	Remove uneaten food	☐	☐	☐	☐	☐	☐	☐
	Check filter	☐	☐	☐	☐	☐	☐	☐
	Check water temperature	☐	☐	☐	☐	☐	☐	☐
🔧	Check other equipment (if used)	☐	☐	☐	☐	☐	☐	☐
🔍	Look for odd behavior & signs of illness or fin damage.	☐	☐	☐	☐	☐	☐	☐

NOTES:

WEEKLY, MONTHLY CHECKLIST

WEEKLY ACTIVITY   DATE: _____

- [ ] Test check water quality once a week
- [ ] Change 1/3 water 2 x week
- [ ] Vacuum up uneaten food and waste.
- [ ] Check pH and bacteria levels.

MONTHLY ACTIVITY   MONTH: _____

- [ ] Check filters, replacing media as necessary
- [ ] Clean fake plants, decorations, & algae
- [ ] Vacuum up all waste & uneaten food from gravel
- [ ] Check water quality & pH levels

HEALTH CHECKLIST   DATE: _____

- Y ☐ N ☐ Active and alert
- Y ☐ N ☐ Eats regularly
- Y ☐ N ☐ Vibrant colors
- Y ☐ N ☐ Undamaged fins
- Y ☐ N ☐ Reacts aggressively to outside stimulus

NOTES:

DAILY CHECKLIST

Activity	WEEK OF						
	SUN	MON	TUE	WED	THU	FRI	SAT
Feed 2-4 pellets, 1 to 2 times daily.	☐	☐	☐	☐	☐	☐	☐
Remove uneaten food	☐	☐	☐	☐	☐	☐	☐
Check filter	☐	☐	☐	☐	☐	☐	☐
Check water temperature	☐	☐	☐	☐	☐	☐	☐
Check other equipment (if used)	☐	☐	☐	☐	☐	☐	☐
Look for odd behavior & signs of illness or fin damage.	☐	☐	☐	☐	☐	☐	☐

NOTES:

WEEKLY, MONTHLY CHECKLIST

WEEKLY ACTIVITY   DATE:

- [ ] Test check water quality once a week
- [ ] Change 1/3 water 2 x week
- [ ] Vacuum up uneaten food and waste.
- [ ] Check pH and bacteria levels.

MONTHLY ACTIVITY   MONTH:

- [ ] Check filters, replacing media as necessary
- [ ] Clean fake plants, decorations, & algae
- [ ] Vacuum up all waste & uneaten food from gravel
- [ ] Check water quality & pH levels

HEALTH CHECKLIST   DATE:

- [ ] Y [ ] N   Active and alert
- [ ] Y [ ] N   Eats regularly
- [ ] Y [ ] N   Vibrant colors
- [ ] Y [ ] N   Undamaged fins
- [ ] Y [ ] N   Reacts aggressively to outside stimulus

NOTES:

DAILY CHECKLIST

📅 Activity	WEEK OF						
	SUN	MON	TUE	WED	THU	FRI	SAT
Feed 2-4 pellets, 1 to 2 times daily.	☐	☐	☐	☐	☐	☐	☐
Remove uneaten food	☐	☐	☐	☐	☐	☐	☐
Check filter	☐	☐	☐	☐	☐	☐	☐
Check water temperature	☐	☐	☐	☐	☐	☐	☐
Check other equipment (if used)	☐	☐	☐	☐	☐	☐	☐
Look for odd behavior & signs of illness or fin damage.	☐	☐	☐	☐	☐	☐	☐

NOTES:

WEEKLY, MONTHLY CHECKLIST

WEEKLY ACTIVITY   DATE:

- [ ] Test check water quality once a week
- [ ] Change 1/3 water 2 x week
- [ ] Vacuum up uneaten food and waste.
- [ ] Check pH and bacteria levels.

MONTHLY ACTIVITY   MONTH:

- [ ] Check filters, replacing media as necessary
- [ ] Clean fake plants, decorations, & algae
- [ ] Vacuum up all waste & uneaten food from gravel
- [ ] Check water quality & pH levels

HEALTH CHECKLIST   DATE:

- Y N Active and alert
- Y N Eats regularly
- Y N Vibrant colors
- Y N Undamaged fins
- Y N Reacts aggressively to outside stimulus

NOTES:

DAILY CHECKLIST

 Activity	WEEK OF
	SUN MON TUE WED THU FRI SAT

	Activity	SUN	MON	TUE	WED	THU	FRI	SAT
	Feed 2-4 pellets, 1 to 2 times daily.	☐	☐	☐	☐	☐	☐	☐
	Remove uneaten food	☐	☐	☐	☐	☐	☐	☐
	Check filter	☐	☐	☐	☐	☐	☐	☐
	Check water temperature	☐	☐	☐	☐	☐	☐	☐
	Check other equipment (if used)	☐	☐	☐	☐	☐	☐	☐
	Look for odd behavior & signs of illness or fin damage.	☐	☐	☐	☐	☐	☐	☐

NOTES:

WEEKLY, MONTHLY CHECKLIST

WEEKLY ACTIVITY   DATE:

- ☐ Test check water quality once a week
- ☐ Change 1/3 water 2 x week
- ☐ Vacuum up uneaten food and waste.
- ☐ Check pH and bacteria levels.

MONTHLY ACTIVITY   MONTH:

- ☐ Check filters, replacing media as necessary
- ☐ Clean fake plants, decorations, & algae
- ☐ Vacuum up all waste & uneaten food from gravel
- ☐ Check water quality & pH levels

HEALTH CHECKLIST   DATE:

- ☐Y ☐N Active and alert
- ☐Y ☐N Eats regularly
- ☐Y ☐N Vibrant colors
- ☐Y ☐N Undamaged fins
- ☐Y ☐N Reacts aggressively to outside stimulus

NOTES:

DAILY CHECKLIST

	Activity	WEEK OF						
		SUN	MON	TUE	WED	THU	FRI	SAT
	Feed 2-4 pellets, 1 to 2 times daily.	☐	☐	☐	☐	☐	☐	☐
	Remove uneaten food	☐	☐	☐	☐	☐	☐	☐
	Check filter	☐	☐	☐	☐	☐	☐	☐
	Check water temperature	☐	☐	☐	☐	☐	☐	☐
	Check other equipment (if used)	☐	☐	☐	☐	☐	☐	☐
	Look for odd behavior & signs of illness or fin damage.	☐	☐	☐	☐	☐	☐	☐

NOTES:

WEEKLY, MONTHLY CHECKLIST

WEEKLY ACTIVITY   DATE:

- [ ] Test check water quality once a week
- [ ] Change 1/3 water 2 x week
- [ ] Vacuum up uneaten food and waste.
- [ ] Check pH and bacteria levels.

MONTHLY ACTIVITY   MONTH:

- [ ] Check filters, replacing media as necessary
- [ ] Clean fake plants, decorations, & algae
- [ ] Vacuum up all waste & uneaten food from gravel
- [ ] Check water quality & pH levels

HEALTH CHECKLIST   DATE:

- [ ] Y [ ] N   Active and alert
- [ ] Y [ ] N   Eats regularly
- [ ] Y [ ] N   Vibrant colors
- [ ] Y [ ] N   Undamaged fins
- [ ] Y [ ] N   Reacts aggressively to outside stimulus

NOTES:

DAILY CHECKLIST

📅 Activity	WEEK OF						
	SUN	MON	TUE	WED	THU	FRI	SAT
Feed 2-4 pellets, 1 to 2 times daily.	☐	☐	☐	☐	☐	☐	☐
Remove uneaten food	☐	☐	☐	☐	☐	☐	☐
Check filter	☐	☐	☐	☐	☐	☐	☐
Check water temperature	☐	☐	☐	☐	☐	☐	☐
Check other equipment (if used)	☐	☐	☐	☐	☐	☐	☐
Look for odd behavior & signs of illness or fin damage.	☐	☐	☐	☐	☐	☐	☐

NOTES:

WEEKLY, MONTHLY CHECKLIST

WEEKLY ACTIVITY   DATE:

- [ ] Test check water quality once a week
- [ ] Change 1/3 water 2 x week
- [ ] Vacuum up uneaten food and waste.
- [ ] Check pH and bacteria levels.

MONTHLY ACTIVITY   MONTH:

- [ ] Check filters, replacing media as necessary
- [ ] Clean fake plants, decorations, & algae
- [ ] Vacuum up all waste & uneaten food from gravel
- [ ] Check water quality & pH levels

HEALTH CHECKLIST   DATE:

- [ ] Y [ ] N   Active and alert
- [ ] Y [ ] N   Eats regularly
- [ ] Y [ ] N   Vibrant colors
- [ ] Y [ ] N   Undamaged fins
- [ ] Y [ ] N   Reacts aggressively to outside stimulus

NOTES:

DAILY CHECKLIST

📅 Activity	WEEK OF
	SUN MON TUE WED THU FRI SAT

Activity	SUN	MON	TUE	WED	THU	FRI	SAT
Feed 2-4 pellets, 1 to 2 times daily.	☐	☐	☐	☐	☐	☐	☐
Remove uneaten food	☐	☐	☐	☐	☐	☐	☐
Check filter	☐	☐	☐	☐	☐	☐	☐
Check water temperature	☐	☐	☐	☐	☐	☐	☐
Check other equipment (if used)	☐	☐	☐	☐	☐	☐	☐
Look for odd behavior & signs of illness or fin damage.	☐	☐	☐	☐	☐	☐	☐

NOTES:

WEEKLY, MONTHLY CHECKLIST

WEEKLY ACTIVITY   DATE:

- [ ] Test check water quality once a week
- [ ] Change 1/3 water 2 x week
- [ ] Vacuum up uneaten food and waste.
- [ ] Check pH and bacteria levels.

MONTHLY ACTIVITY   MONTH:

- [ ] Check filters, replacing media as necessary
- [ ] Clean fake plants, decorations, & algae
- [ ] Vacuum up all waste & uneaten food from gravel
- [ ] Check water quality & pH levels

HEALTH CHECKLIST   DATE:

- Y [ ] N [ ] Active and alert
- Y [ ] N [ ] Eats regularly
- Y [ ] N [ ] Vibrant colors
- Y [ ] N [ ] Undamaged fins
- Y [ ] N [ ] Reacts aggressively to outside stimulus

NOTES:

DAILY CHECKLIST

📅 Activity	WEEK OF _____
	SUN MON TUE WED THU FRI SAT

Activity	SUN	MON	TUE	WED	THU	FRI	SAT
Feed 2-4 pellets, 1 to 2 times daily.	☐	☐	☐	☐	☐	☐	☐
Remove uneaten food	☐	☐	☐	☐	☐	☐	☐
Check filter	☐	☐	☐	☐	☐	☐	☐
Check water temperature	☐	☐	☐	☐	☐	☐	☐
Check other equipment (if used)	☐	☐	☐	☐	☐	☐	☐
Look for odd behavior & signs of illness or fin damage.	☐	☐	☐	☐	☐	☐	☐

NOTES:

WEEKLY, MONTHLY CHECKLIST

WEEKLY ACTIVITY   DATE: _____

- [ ] Test check water quality once a week
- [ ] Change 1/3 water 2 x week
- [ ] Vacuum up uneaten food and waste.
- [ ] Check pH and bacteria levels.

MONTHLY ACTIVITY   MONTH: _____

- [ ] Check filters, replacing media as necessary
- [ ] Clean fake plants, decorations, & algae
- [ ] Vacuum up all waste & uneaten food from gravel
- [ ] Check water quality & pH levels

HEALTH CHECKLIST   DATE: _____

- [ ] Y [ ] N   Active and alert
- [ ] Y [ ] N   Eats regularly
- [ ] Y [ ] N   Vibrant colors
- [ ] Y [ ] N   Undamaged fins
- [ ] Y [ ] N   Reacts aggressively to outside stimulus

NOTES:

DAILY CHECKLIST

Activity	WEEK OF						
	SUN	MON	TUE	WED	THU	FRI	SAT
Feed 2-4 pellets, 1 to 2 times daily.	☐	☐	☐	☐	☐	☐	☐
Remove uneaten food	☐	☐	☐	☐	☐	☐	☐
Check filter	☐	☐	☐	☐	☐	☐	☐
Check water temperature	☐	☐	☐	☐	☐	☐	☐
Check other equipment (if used)	☐	☐	☐	☐	☐	☐	☐
Look for odd behavior & signs of illness or fin damage.	☐	☐	☐	☐	☐	☐	☐

NOTES:

WEEKLY, MONTHLY CHECKLIST

- [ ] Test check water quality once a week
- [ ] Change 1/3 water 2 x week
- [ ] Vacuum up uneaten food and waste.
- [ ] Check pH and bacteria levels.

MONTHLY ACTIVITY   MONTH:

- [ ] Check filters, replacing media as necessary
- [ ] Clean fake plants, decorations, & algae
- [ ] Vacuum up all waste & uneaten food from gravel
- [ ] Check water quality & pH levels

HEALTH CHECKLIST   DATE:

- [Y] [N] Active and alert
- [Y] [N] Eats regularly
- [Y] [N] Vibrant colors
- [Y] [N] Undamaged fins
- [Y] [N] Reacts aggressively to outside stimulus

NOTES:

DAILY CHECKLIST

Activity	WEEK OF						
	SUN	MON	TUE	WED	THU	FRI	SAT
Feed 2-4 pellets, 1 to 2 times daily.	☐	☐	☐	☐	☐	☐	☐
Remove uneaten food	☐	☐	☐	☐	☐	☐	☐
Check filter	☐	☐	☐	☐	☐	☐	☐
Check water temperature	☐	☐	☐	☐	☐	☐	☐
Check other equipment (if used)	☐	☐	☐	☐	☐	☐	☐
Look for odd behavior & signs of illness or fin damage.	☐	☐	☐	☐	☐	☐	☐

NOTES:

WEEKLY, MONTHLY CHECKLIST

- ☐ Test check water quality once a week
- ☐ Change 1/3 water 2 x week
- ☐ Vacuum up uneaten food and waste.
- ☐ Check pH and bacteria levels.

MONTHLY ACTIVITY   MONTH:

- ☐ Check filters, replacing media as necessary
- ☐ Clean fake plants, decorations, & algae
- ☐ Vacuum up all waste & uneaten food from gravel
- ☐ Check water quality & pH levels

HEALTH CHECKLIST   DATE:

- ☐ Y ☐ N Active and alert
- ☐ Y ☐ N Eats regularly
- ☐ Y ☐ N Vibrant colors
- ☐ Y ☐ N Undamaged fins
- ☐ Y ☐ N Reacts aggressively to outside stimulus

NOTES:

DAILY CHECKLIST

Activity	SUN	MON	TUE	WED	THU	FRI	SAT

WEEK OF _____

	SUN	MON	TUE	WED	THU	FRI	SAT
Feed 2-4 pellets, 1 to 2 times daily.	☐	☐	☐	☐	☐	☐	☐
Remove uneaten food	☐	☐	☐	☐	☐	☐	☐
Check filter	☐	☐	☐	☐	☐	☐	☐
Check water temperature	☐	☐	☐	☐	☐	☐	☐
Check other equipment (if used)	☐	☐	☐	☐	☐	☐	☐
Look for odd behavior & signs of illness or fin damage.	☐	☐	☐	☐	☐	☐	☐

NOTES: _____

WEEKLY, MONTHLY CHECKLIST

WEEKLY ACTIVITY   DATE: [ ]

- ☐ Test check water quality once a week
- ☐ Change 1/3 water 2 x week
- ☐ Vacuum up uneaten food and waste.
- ☐ Check pH and bacteria levels.

MONTHLY ACTIVITY   MONTH: [ ]

- ☐ Check filters, replacing media as necessary
- ☐ Clean fake plants, decorations, & algae
- ☐ Vacuum up all waste & uneaten food from gravel
- ☐ Check water quality & pH levels

HEALTH CHECKLIST   DATE: [ ]

- Y ☐ N ☐ Active and alert
- Y ☐ N ☐ Eats regularly
- Y ☐ N ☐ Vibrant colors
- Y ☐ N ☐ Undamaged fins
- Y ☐ N ☐ Reacts aggressively to outside stimulus

NOTES:

DAILY CHECKLIST

Activity	WEEK OF
	SUN MON TUE WED THU FRI SAT
Feed 2-4 pellets, 1 to 2 times daily.	☐ ☐ ☐ ☐ ☐ ☐ ☐
Remove uneaten food	☐ ☐ ☐ ☐ ☐ ☐ ☐
Check filter	☐ ☐ ☐ ☐ ☐ ☐ ☐
Check water temperature	☐ ☐ ☐ ☐ ☐ ☐ ☐
Check other equipment (if used)	☐ ☐ ☐ ☐ ☐ ☐ ☐
Look for odd behavior & signs of illness or fin damage.	☐ ☐ ☐ ☐ ☐ ☐ ☐

NOTES:

WEEKLY, MONTHLY CHECKLIST

WEEKLY ACTIVITY   DATE: [____]

- [ ] Test check water quality once a week
- [ ] Change 1/3 water 2 x week
- [ ] Vacuum up uneaten food and waste.
- [ ] Check pH and bacteria levels.

MONTHLY ACTIVITY   MONTH: [____]

- [ ] Check filters, replacing media as necessary
- [ ] Clean fake plants, decorations, & algae
- [ ] Vacuum up all waste & uneaten food from gravel
- [ ] Check water quality & pH levels

HEALTH CHECKLIST   DATE: [____]

- Y / N   Active and alert
- Y / N   Eats regularly
- Y / N   Vibrant colors
- Y / N   Undamaged fins
- Y / N   Reacts aggressively to outside stimulus

NOTES:

DAILY CHECKLIST

Activity	WEEK OF						
	SUN	MON	TUE	WED	THU	FRI	SAT
Feed 2-4 pellets, 1 to 2 times daily.	☐	☐	☐	☐	☐	☐	☐
Remove uneaten food	☐	☐	☐	☐	☐	☐	☐
Check filter	☐	☐	☐	☐	☐	☐	☐
Check water temperature	☐	☐	☐	☐	☐	☐	☐
Check other equipment (if used)	☐	☐	☐	☐	☐	☐	☐
Look for odd behavior & signs of illness or fin damage.	☐	☐	☐	☐	☐	☐	☐

NOTES:

WEEKLY, MONTHLY CHECKLIST

- ☐ Test check water quality once a week
- ☐ Change 1/3 water 2 x week
- ☐ Vacuum up uneaten food and waste.
- ☐ Check pH and bacteria levels.

MONTHLY ACTIVITY   MONTH:

- ☐ Check filters, replacing media as necessary
- ☐ Clean fake plants, decorations, & algae
- ☐ Vacuum up all waste & uneaten food from gravel
- ☐ Check water quality & pH levels

- ☐ Y ☐ N Active and alert
- ☐ Y ☐ N Eats regularly
- ☐ Y ☐ N Vibrant colors
- ☐ Y ☐ N Undamaged fins
- ☐ Y ☐ N Reacts aggressively to outside stimulus

NOTES:

DAILY CHECKLIST

Activity	WEEK OF	SUN	MON	TUE	WED	THU	FRI	SAT
Feed 2-4 pellets, 1 to 2 times daily.		☐	☐	☐	☐	☐	☐	☐
Remove uneaten food		☐	☐	☐	☐	☐	☐	☐
Check filter		☐	☐	☐	☐	☐	☐	☐
Check water temperature		☐	☐	☐	☐	☐	☐	☐
Check other equipment (if used)		☐	☐	☐	☐	☐	☐	☐
Look for odd behavior & signs of illness or fin damage.		☐	☐	☐	☐	☐	☐	☐

NOTES:

WEEKLY, MONTHLY CHECKLIST

WEEKLY ACTIVITY   DATE:

- ☐ Test check water quality once a week
- ☐ Change 1/3 water 2 x week
- ☐ Vacuum up uneaten food and waste.
- ☐ Check pH and bacteria levels.

MONTHLY ACTIVITY   MONTH:

- ☐ Check filters, replacing media as necessary
- ☐ Clean fake plants, decorations, & algae
- ☐ Vacuum up all waste & uneaten food from gravel
- ☐ Check water quality & pH levels

HEALTH CHECKLIST   DATE:

- ☐ Y ☐ N   Active and alert
- ☐ Y ☐ N   Eats regularly
- ☐ Y ☐ N   Vibrant colors
- ☐ Y ☐ N   Undamaged fins
- ☐ Y ☐ N   Reacts aggressively to outside stimulus

NOTES:

DAILY CHECKLIST

Activity	WEEK OF						
	SUN	MON	TUE	WED	THU	FRI	SAT
Feed 2-4 pellets, 1 to 2 times daily.	☐	☐	☐	☐	☐	☐	☐
Remove uneaten food	☐	☐	☐	☐	☐	☐	☐
Check filter	☐	☐	☐	☐	☐	☐	☐
Check water temperature	☐	☐	☐	☐	☐	☐	☐
Check other equipment (if used)	☐	☐	☐	☐	☐	☐	☐
Look for odd behavior & signs of illness or fin damage.	☐	☐	☐	☐	☐	☐	☐

NOTES:

WEEKLY, MONTHLY CHECKLIST

WEEKLY ACTIVITY   DATE: [ ]

- [ ] Test check water quality once a week
- [ ] Change 1/3 water 2 x week
- [ ] Vacuum up uneaten food and waste.
- [ ] Check pH and bacteria levels.

MONTHLY ACTIVITY   MONTH:

- [ ] Check filters, replacing media as necessary
- [ ] Clean fake plants, decorations, & algae
- [ ] Vacuum up all waste & uneaten food from gravel
- [ ] Check water quality & pH levels

HEALTH CHECKLIST   DATE: [ ]

- [Y] [N] Active and alert
- [Y] [N] Eats regularly
- [Y] [N] Vibrant colors
- [Y] [N] Undamaged fins
- [Y] [N] Reacts aggressively to outside stimulus

NOTES:

DAILY CHECKLIST

	Activity	WEEK OF						
		SUN	MON	TUE	WED	THU	FRI	SAT
	Feed 2-4 pellets, 1 to 2 times daily.	☐	☐	☐	☐	☐	☐	☐
	Remove uneaten food	☐	☐	☐	☐	☐	☐	☐
	Check filter	☐	☐	☐	☐	☐	☐	☐
	Check water temperature	☐	☐	☐	☐	☐	☐	☐
	Check other equipment (if used)	☐	☐	☐	☐	☐	☐	☐
	Look for odd behavior & signs of illness or fin damage.	☐	☐	☐	☐	☐	☐	☐

NOTES:

WEEKLY, MONTHLY CHECKLIST

- ☐ Test check water quality once a week
- ☐ Change 1/3 water 2 x week
- ☐ Vacuum up uneaten food and waste.
- ☐ Check pH and bacteria levels.

MONTHLY ACTIVITY   MONTH:

- ☐ Check filters, replacing media as necessary
- ☐ Clean fake plants, decorations, & algae
- ☐ Vacuum up all waste & uneaten food from gravel
- ☐ Check water quality & pH levels

- ☐ Y ☐ N Active and alert
- ☐ Y ☐ N Eats regularly
- ☐ Y ☐ N Vibrant colors
- ☐ Y ☐ N Undamaged fins
- ☐ Y ☐ N Reacts aggressively to outside stimulus

NOTES:

DAILY CHECKLIST

📅 Activity	WEEK OF						
	SUN	MON	TUE	WED	THU	FRI	SAT
Feed 2-4 pellets, 1 to 2 times daily.	☐	☐	☐	☐	☐	☐	☐
Remove uneaten food	☐	☐	☐	☐	☐	☐	☐
Check filter	☐	☐	☐	☐	☐	☐	☐
Check water temperature	☐	☐	☐	☐	☐	☐	☐
Check other equipment (if used)	☐	☐	☐	☐	☐	☐	☐
Look for odd behavior & signs of illness or fin damage.	☐	☐	☐	☐	☐	☐	☐

NOTES:

WEEKLY, MONTHLY CHECKLIST

WEEKLY ACTIVITY   DATE:

- [ ] Test check water quality once a week
- [ ] Change 1/3 water 2 x week
- [ ] Vacuum up uneaten food and waste.
- [ ] Check pH and bacteria levels.

MONTHLY ACTIVITY   MONTH:

- [ ] Check filters, replacing media as necessary
- [ ] Clean fake plants, decorations, & algae
- [ ] Vacuum up all waste & uneaten food from gravel
- [ ] Check water quality & pH levels

HEALTH CHECKLIST   DATE:

- Y / N   Active and alert
- Y / N   Eats regularly
- Y / N   Vibrant colors
- Y / N   Undamaged fins
- Y / N   Reacts aggressively to outside stimulus

NOTES:

DAILY CHECKLIST

Activity	WEEK OF	SUN	MON	TUE	WED	THU	FRI	SAT
Feed 2-4 pellets, 1 to 2 times daily.		☐	☐	☐	☐	☐	☐	☐
Remove uneaten food		☐	☐	☐	☐	☐	☐	☐
Check filter		☐	☐	☐	☐	☐	☐	☐
Check water temperature		☐	☐	☐	☐	☐	☐	☐
Check other equipment (if used)		☐	☐	☐	☐	☐	☐	☐
Look for odd behavior & signs of illness or fin damage.		☐	☐	☐	☐	☐	☐	☐

NOTES:

WEEKLY, MONTHLY CHECKLIST

WEEKLY ACTIVITY   DATE:

- [ ] Test check water quality once a week
- [ ] Change 1/3 water 2 x week
- [ ] Vacuum up uneaten food and waste.
- [ ] Check pH and bacteria levels.

MONTHLY ACTIVITY   MONTH:

- [ ] Check filters, replacing media as necessary
- [ ] Clean fake plants, decorations, & algae
- [ ] Vacuum up all waste & uneaten food from gravel
- [ ] Check water quality & pH levels

HEALTH CHECKLIST   DATE:

- Y / N Active and alert
- Y / N Eats regularly
- Y / N Vibrant colors
- Y / N Undamaged fins
- Y / N Reacts aggressively to outside stimulus

NOTES:

DAILY CHECKLIST

Activity	WEEK OF						
	SUN	MON	TUE	WED	THU	FRI	SAT
Feed 2-4 pellets, 1 to 2 times daily.	☐	☐	☐	☐	☐	☐	☐
Remove uneaten food	☐	☐	☐	☐	☐	☐	☐
Check filter	☐	☐	☐	☐	☐	☐	☐
Check water temperature	☐	☐	☐	☐	☐	☐	☐
Check other equipment (if used)	☐	☐	☐	☐	☐	☐	☐
Look for odd behavior & signs of illness or fin damage.	☐	☐	☐	☐	☐	☐	☐

NOTES:

WEEKLY, MONTHLY CHECKLIST

WEEKLY ACTIVITY DATE:

- ☐ Test check water quality once a week
- ☐ Change 1/3 water 2 x week
- ☐ Vacuum up uneaten food and waste.
- ☐ Check pH and bacteria levels.

MONTHLY ACTIVITY MONTH:

- ☐ Check filters, replacing media as necessary
- ☐ Clean fake plants, decorations, & algae
- ☐ Vacuum up all waste & uneaten food from gravel
- ☐ Check water quality & pH levels

HEALTH CHECKLIST DATE:

- ☐Y ☐N Active and alert
- ☐Y ☐N Eats regularly
- ☐Y ☐N Vibrant colors
- ☐Y ☐N Undamaged fins
- ☐Y ☐N Reacts aggressively to outside stimulus

NOTES:

DAILY CHECKLIST

📅 Activity	WEEK OF						
	SUN	MON	TUE	WED	THU	FRI	SAT
Feed 2-4 pellets, 1 to 2 times daily.	☐	☐	☐	☐	☐	☐	☐
Remove uneaten food	☐	☐	☐	☐	☐	☐	☐
Check filter	☐	☐	☐	☐	☐	☐	☐
Check water temperature	☐	☐	☐	☐	☐	☐	☐
Check other equipment (if used)	☐	☐	☐	☐	☐	☐	☐
Look for odd behavior & signs of illness or fin damage.	☐	☐	☐	☐	☐	☐	☐

NOTES:

WEEKLY, MONTHLY CHECKLIST

WEEKLY ACTIVITY   DATE:

- ☐ Test check water quality once a week
- ☐ Change 1/3 water 2 x week
- ☐ Vacuum up uneaten food and waste.
- ☐ Check pH and bacteria levels.

MONTHLY ACTIVITY   MONTH:

- ☐ Check filters, replacing media as necessary
- ☐ Clean fake plants, decorations, & algae
- ☐ Vacuum up all waste & uneaten food from gravel
- ☐ Check water quality & pH levels

HEALTH CHECKLIST   DATE:

- ☐ Y ☐ N Active and alert
- ☐ Y ☐ N Eats regularly
- ☐ Y ☐ N Vibrant colors
- ☐ Y ☐ N Undamaged fins
- ☐ Y ☐ N Reacts aggressively to outside stimulus

NOTES:

DAILY CHECKLIST

Activity	WEEK OF						
	SUN	MON	TUE	WED	THU	FRI	SAT
Feed 2-4 pellets, 1 to 2 times daily.	☐	☐	☐	☐	☐	☐	☐
Remove uneaten food	☐	☐	☐	☐	☐	☐	☐
Check filter	☐	☐	☐	☐	☐	☐	☐
Check water temperature	☐	☐	☐	☐	☐	☐	☐
Check other equipment (if used)	☐	☐	☐	☐	☐	☐	☐
Look for odd behavior & signs of illness or fin damage.	☐	☐	☐	☐	☐	☐	☐

NOTES:

WEEKLY, MONTHLY CHECKLIST

WEEKLY ACTIVITY   DATE:

- [ ] Test check water quality once a week
- [ ] Change 1/3 water 2 x week
- [ ] Vacuum up uneaten food and waste.
- [ ] Check pH and bacteria levels.

MONTHLY ACTIVITY   MONTH:

- [ ] Check filters, replacing media as necessary
- [ ] Clean fake plants, decorations, & algae
- [ ] Vacuum up all waste & uneaten food from gravel
- [ ] Check water quality & pH levels

HEALTH CHECKLIST   DATE:

- [Y] [N] Active and alert
- [Y] [N] Eats regularly
- [Y] [N] Vibrant colors
- [Y] [N] Undamaged fins
- [Y] [N] Reacts aggressively to outside stimulus

NOTES:

DAILY CHECKLIST

Activity	WEEK OF						
	SUN	MON	TUE	WED	THU	FRI	SAT
Feed 2-4 pellets, 1 to 2 times daily.	☐	☐	☐	☐	☐	☐	☐
Remove uneaten food	☐	☐	☐	☐	☐	☐	☐
Check filter	☐	☐	☐	☐	☐	☐	☐
Check water temperature	☐	☐	☐	☐	☐	☐	☐
Check other equipment (if used)	☐	☐	☐	☐	☐	☐	☐
Look for odd behavior & signs of illness or fin damage.	☐	☐	☐	☐	☐	☐	☐

NOTES:

WEEKLY, MONTHLY CHECKLIST

WEEKLY ACTIVITY   DATE:

- [ ] Test check water quality once a week
- [ ] Change 1/3 water 2 x week
- [ ] Vacuum up uneaten food and waste.
- [ ] Check pH and bacteria levels.

MONTHLY ACTIVITY   MONTH:

- [ ] Check filters, replacing media as necessary
- [ ] Clean fake plants, decorations, & algae
- [ ] Vacuum up all waste & uneaten food from gravel
- [ ] Check water quality & pH levels

HEALTH CHECKLIST   DATE:

- [ ] Y [ ] N   Active and alert
- [ ] Y [ ] N   Eats regularly
- [ ] Y [ ] N   Vibrant colors
- [ ] Y [ ] N   Undamaged fins
- [ ] Y [ ] N   Reacts aggressively to outside stimulus

NOTES:

DAILY CHECKLIST

Activity	WEEK OF						
	SUN	MON	TUE	WED	THU	FRI	SAT
Feed 2-4 pellets, 1 to 2 times daily.	☐	☐	☐	☐	☐	☐	☐
Remove uneaten food	☐	☐	☐	☐	☐	☐	☐
Check filter	☐	☐	☐	☐	☐	☐	☐
Check water temperature	☐	☐	☐	☐	☐	☐	☐
Check other equipment (if used)	☐	☐	☐	☐	☐	☐	☐
Look for odd behavior & signs of illness or fin damage.	☐	☐	☐	☐	☐	☐	☐

NOTES:

WEEKLY, MONTHLY CHECKLIST

WEEKLY ACTIVITY   DATE:

- [ ] Test check water quality once a week
- [ ] Change 1/3 water 2 x week
- [ ] Vacuum up uneaten food and waste.
- [ ] Check pH and bacteria levels.

MONTHLY ACTIVITY   MONTH:

- [ ] Check filters, replacing media as necessary
- [ ] Clean fake plants, decorations, & algae
- [ ] Vacuum up all waste & uneaten food from gravel
- [ ] Check water quality & pH levels

HEALTH CHECKLIST   DATE:

- [ ] Y [ ] N Active and alert
- [ ] Y [ ] N Eats regularly
- [ ] Y [ ] N Vibrant colors
- [ ] Y [ ] N Undamaged fins
- [ ] Y [ ] N Reacts aggressively to outside stimulus

NOTES:

DAILY CHECKLIST

📅 Activity	WEEK OF						
	SUN	MON	TUE	WED	THU	FRI	SAT
Feed 2-4 pellets, 1 to 2 times daily.	☐	☐	☐	☐	☐	☐	☐
Remove uneaten food	☐	☐	☐	☐	☐	☐	☐
Check filter	☐	☐	☐	☐	☐	☐	☐
Check water temperature	☐	☐	☐	☐	☐	☐	☐
Check other equipment (if used)	☐	☐	☐	☐	☐	☐	☐
Look for odd behavior & signs of illness or fin damage.	☐	☐	☐	☐	☐	☐	☐

NOTES:

WEEKLY, MONTHLY CHECKLIST

WEEKLY ACTIVITY   DATE: [   ]

- [ ] Test check water quality once a week
- [ ] Change 1/3 water 2 x week
- [ ] Vacuum up uneaten food and waste.
- [ ] Check pH and bacteria levels.

MONTHLY ACTIVITY   MONTH:

- [ ] Check filters, replacing media as necessary
- [ ] Clean fake plants, decorations, & algae
- [ ] Vacuum up all waste & uneaten food from gravel
- [ ] Check water quality & pH levels

HEALTH CHECKLIST   DATE: [   ]

- Y / N Active and alert
- Y / N Eats regularly
- Y / N Vibrant colors
- Y / N Undamaged fins
- Y / N Reacts aggressively to outside stimulus

NOTES:

DAILY CHECKLIST

Activity	WEEK OF						
	SUN	MON	TUE	WED	THU	FRI	SAT
Feed 2-4 pellets, 1 to 2 times daily.	☐	☐	☐	☐	☐	☐	☐
Remove uneaten food	☐	☐	☐	☐	☐	☐	☐
Check filter	☐	☐	☐	☐	☐	☐	☐
Check water temperature	☐	☐	☐	☐	☐	☐	☐
Check other equipment (if used)	☐	☐	☐	☐	☐	☐	☐
Look for odd behavior & signs of illness or fin damage.	☐	☐	☐	☐	☐	☐	☐

NOTES:

WEEKLY, MONTHLY CHECKLIST

WEEKLY ACTIVITY   DATE: _____

- [ ] Test check water quality once a week
- [ ] Change 1/3 water 2 x week
- [ ] Vacuum up uneaten food and waste.
- [ ] Check pH and bacteria levels.

MONTHLY ACTIVITY   MONTH: _____

- [ ] Check filters, replacing media as necessary
- [ ] Clean fake plants, decorations, & algae
- [ ] Vacuum up all waste & uneaten food from gravel
- [ ] Check water quality & pH levels

HEALTH CHECKLIST   DATE: _____

- Y ☐ N ☐ Active and alert
- Y ☐ N ☐ Eats regularly
- Y ☐ N ☐ Vibrant colors
- Y ☐ N ☐ Undamaged fins
- Y ☐ N ☐ Reacts aggressively to outside stimulus

NOTES:

DAILY CHECKLIST

Activity	WEEK OF ☐
	SUN MON TUE WED THU FRI SAT

	Activity	SUN	MON	TUE	WED	THU	FRI	SAT
	Feed 2-4 pellets, 1 to 2 times daily.	☐	☐	☐	☐	☐	☐	☐
	Remove uneaten food	☐	☐	☐	☐	☐	☐	☐
	Check filter	☐	☐	☐	☐	☐	☐	☐
	Check water temperature	☐	☐	☐	☐	☐	☐	☐
	Check other equipment (if used)	☐	☐	☐	☐	☐	☐	☐
	Look for odd behavior & signs of illness or fin damage.	☐	☐	☐	☐	☐	☐	☐

NOTES:

WEEKLY, MONTHLY CHECKLIST

WEEKLY ACTIVITY DATE:

- [ ] Test check water quality once a week
- [ ] Change 1/3 water 2 x week
- [ ] Vacuum up uneaten food and waste.
- [ ] Check pH and bacteria levels.

MONTHLY ACTIVITY MONTH:

- [ ] Check filters, replacing media as necessary
- [ ] Clean fake plants, decorations, & algae
- [ ] Vacuum up all waste & uneaten food from gravel
- [ ] Check water quality & pH levels

HEALTH CHECKLIST DATE:

- Y N Active and alert
- Y N Eats regularly
- Y N Vibrant colors
- Y N Undamaged fins
- Y N Reacts aggressively to outside stimulus

NOTES:

DAILY CHECKLIST

Activity	WEEK OF	SUN	MON	TUE	WED	THU	FRI	SAT
Feed 2-4 pellets, 1 to 2 times daily.		☐	☐	☐	☐	☐	☐	☐
Remove uneaten food		☐	☐	☐	☐	☐	☐	☐
Check filter		☐	☐	☐	☐	☐	☐	☐
Check water temperature		☐	☐	☐	☐	☐	☐	☐
Check other equipment (if used)		☐	☐	☐	☐	☐	☐	☐
Look for odd behavior & signs of illness or fin damage.		☐	☐	☐	☐	☐	☐	☐

NOTES:

WEEKLY, MONTHLY CHECKLIST

WEEKLY ACTIVITY   DATE:

- [ ] Test check water quality once a week
- [ ] Change 1/3 water 2 x week
- [ ] Vacuum up uneaten food and waste.
- [ ] Check pH and bacteria levels.

MONTHLY ACTIVITY   MONTH:

- [ ] Check filters, replacing media as necessary
- [ ] Clean fake plants, decorations, & algae
- [ ] Vacuum up all waste & uneaten food from gravel
- [ ] Check water quality & pH levels

HEALTH CHECKLIST   DATE:

- Y / N   Active and alert
- Y / N   Eats regularly
- Y / N   Vibrant colors
- Y / N   Undamaged fins
- Y / N   Reacts aggressively to outside stimulus

NOTES:

DAILY CHECKLIST

Activity	WEEK OF						
	SUN	MON	TUE	WED	THU	FRI	SAT
Feed 2-4 pellets, 1 to 2 times daily.	☐	☐	☐	☐	☐	☐	☐
Remove uneaten food	☐	☐	☐	☐	☐	☐	☐
Check filter	☐	☐	☐	☐	☐	☐	☐
Check water temperature	☐	☐	☐	☐	☐	☐	☐
Check other equipment (if used)	☐	☐	☐	☐	☐	☐	☐
Look for odd behavior & signs of illness or fin damage.	☐	☐	☐	☐	☐	☐	☐

NOTES:

WEEKLY, MONTHLY CHECKLIST

WEEKLY ACTIVITY   DATE:

- [ ] Test check water quality once a week
- [ ] Change 1/3 water 2 x week
- [ ] Vacuum up uneaten food and waste.
- [ ] Check pH and bacteria levels.

MONTHLY ACTIVITY   MONTH:

- [ ] Check filters, replacing media as necessary
- [ ] Clean fake plants, decorations, & algae
- [ ] Vacuum up all waste & uneaten food from gravel
- [ ] Check water quality & pH levels

HEALTH CHECKLIST   DATE:

- Y / N Active and alert
- Y / N Eats regularly
- Y / N Vibrant colors
- Y / N Undamaged fins
- Y / N Reacts aggressively to outside stimulus

NOTES:

DAILY CHECKLIST

Activity	WEEK OF						
	SUN	MON	TUE	WED	THU	FRI	SAT
Feed 2-4 pellets, 1 to 2 times daily.	☐	☐	☐	☐	☐	☐	☐
Remove uneaten food	☐	☐	☐	☐	☐	☐	☐
Check filter	☐	☐	☐	☐	☐	☐	☐
Check water temperature	☐	☐	☐	☐	☐	☐	☐
Check other equipment (if used)	☐	☐	☐	☐	☐	☐	☐
Look for odd behavior & signs of illness or fin damage.	☐	☐	☐	☐	☐	☐	☐

NOTES:

WEEKLY, MONTHLY CHECKLIST

WEEKLY ACTIVITY DATE: ____

- [ ] Test check water quality once a week
- [ ] Change 1/3 water 2 x week
- [ ] Vacuum up uneaten food and waste.
- [ ] Check pH and bacteria levels.

MONTHLY ACTIVITY MONTH: ____

- [ ] Check filters, replacing media as necessary
- [ ] Clean fake plants, decorations, & algae
- [ ] Vacuum up all waste & uneaten food from gravel
- [ ] Check water quality & pH levels

HEALTH CHECKLIST DATE: ____

- [Y] [N] Active and alert
- [Y] [N] Eats regularly
- [Y] [N] Vibrant colors
- [Y] [N] Undamaged fins
- [Y] [N] Reacts aggressively to outside stimulus

NOTES:

DAILY CHECKLIST

Activity	WEEK OF						
	SUN	MON	TUE	WED	THU	FRI	SAT
Feed 2-4 pellets, 1 to 2 times daily.	☐	☐	☐	☐	☐	☐	☐
Remove uneaten food	☐	☐	☐	☐	☐	☐	☐
Check filter	☐	☐	☐	☐	☐	☐	☐
Check water temperature	☐	☐	☐	☐	☐	☐	☐
Check other equipment (if used)	☐	☐	☐	☐	☐	☐	☐
Look for odd behavior & signs of illness or fin damage.	☐	☐	☐	☐	☐	☐	☐

NOTES:

WEEKLY, MONTHLY CHECKLIST

WEEKLY ACTIVITY DATE:

- [ ] Test check water quality once a week
- [ ] Change 1/3 water 2 x week
- [ ] Vacuum up uneaten food and waste.
- [ ] Check pH and bacteria levels.

MONTHLY ACTIVITY MONTH:

- [ ] Check filters, replacing media as necessary
- [ ] Clean fake plants, decorations, & algae
- [ ] Vacuum up all waste & uneaten food from gravel
- [ ] Check water quality & pH levels

HEALTH CHECKLIST DATE:

- [Y] [N] Active and alert
- [Y] [N] Eats regularly
- [Y] [N] Vibrant colors
- [Y] [N] Undamaged fins
- [Y] [N] Reacts aggressively to outside stimulus

NOTES:

DAILY CHECKLIST

📅 Activity	WEEK OF						
	SUN	MON	TUE	WED	THU	FRI	SAT
Feed 2-4 pellets, 1 to 2 times daily.	☐	☐	☐	☐	☐	☐	☐
Remove uneaten food	☐	☐	☐	☐	☐	☐	☐
Check filter	☐	☐	☐	☐	☐	☐	☐
Check water temperature	☐	☐	☐	☐	☐	☐	☐
Check other equipment (if used)	☐	☐	☐	☐	☐	☐	☐
Look for odd behavior & signs of illness or fin damage.	☐	☐	☐	☐	☐	☐	☐

NOTES:

WEEKLY, MONTHLY CHECKLIST

- ☐ Test check water quality once a week
- ☐ Change 1/3 water 2 x week
- ☐ Vacuum up uneaten food and waste.
- ☐ Check pH and bacteria levels.

MONTHLY ACTIVITY   MONTH:

- ☐ Check filters, replacing media as necessary
- ☐ Clean fake plants, decorations, & algae
- ☐ Vacuum up all waste & uneaten food from gravel
- ☐ Check water quality & pH levels

HEALTH CHECKLIST   DATE:

- ☐ Y ☐ N   Active and alert
- ☐ Y ☐ N   Eats regularly
- ☐ Y ☐ N   Vibrant colors
- ☐ Y ☐ N   Undamaged fins
- ☐ Y ☐ N   Reacts aggressively to outside stimulus

NOTES:

DAILY CHECKLIST

Activity		SUN	MON	TUE	WED	THU	FRI	SAT
	WEEK OF							
Feed 2-4 pellets, 1 to 2 times daily.		☐	☐	☐	☐	☐	☐	☐
Remove uneaten food		☐	☐	☐	☐	☐	☐	☐
Check filter		☐	☐	☐	☐	☐	☐	☐
Check water temperature		☐	☐	☐	☐	☐	☐	☐
Check other equipment (if used)		☐	☐	☐	☐	☐	☐	☐
Look for odd behavior & signs of illness or fin damage.		☐	☐	☐	☐	☐	☐	☐

NOTES:

WEEKLY, MONTHLY CHECKLIST

WEEKLY ACTIVITY   DATE:

- [ ] Test check water quality once a week
- [ ] Change 1/3 water 2 x week
- [ ] Vacuum up uneaten food and waste.
- [ ] Check pH and bacteria levels.

MONTHLY ACTIVITY   MONTH:

- [ ] Check filters, replacing media as necessary
- [ ] Clean fake plants, decorations, & algae
- [ ] Vacuum up all waste & uneaten food from gravel
- [ ] Check water quality & pH levels

HEALTH CHECKLIST   DATE:

- Y N Active and alert
- Y N Eats regularly
- Y N Vibrant colors
- Y N Undamaged fins
- Y N Reacts aggressively to outside stimulus

NOTES:

DAILY CHECKLIST

Activity	WEEK OF						
	SUN	MON	TUE	WED	THU	FRI	SAT
Feed 2-4 pellets, 1 to 2 times daily.	☐	☐	☐	☐	☐	☐	☐
Remove uneaten food	☐	☐	☐	☐	☐	☐	☐
Check filter	☐	☐	☐	☐	☐	☐	☐
Check water temperature	☐	☐	☐	☐	☐	☐	☐
Check other equipment (if used)	☐	☐	☐	☐	☐	☐	☐
Look for odd behavior & signs of illness or fin damage.	☐	☐	☐	☐	☐	☐	☐

NOTES:

WEEKLY, MONTHLY CHECKLIST

WEEKLY ACTIVITY   DATE: [   ]

- [ ] Test check water quality once a week
- [ ] Change 1/3 water 2 x week
- [ ] Vacuum up uneaten food and waste.
- [ ] Check pH and bacteria levels.

MONTHLY ACTIVITY   MONTH: [   ]

- [ ] Check filters, replacing media as necessary
- [ ] Clean fake plants, decorations, & algae
- [ ] Vacuum up all waste & uneaten food from gravel
- [ ] Check water quality & pH levels

HEALTH CHECKLIST   DATE: [   ]

- [ ] Y [ ] N   Active and alert
- [ ] Y [ ] N   Eats regularly
- [ ] Y [ ] N   Vibrant colors
- [ ] Y [ ] N   Undamaged fins
- [ ] Y [ ] N   Reacts aggressively to outside stimulus

NOTES:

DAILY CHECKLIST

Activity	WEEK OF						
	SUN	MON	TUE	WED	THU	FRI	SAT
Feed 2-4 pellets, 1 to 2 times daily.	☐	☐	☐	☐	☐	☐	☐
Remove uneaten food	☐	☐	☐	☐	☐	☐	☐
Check filter	☐	☐	☐	☐	☐	☐	☐
Check water temperature	☐	☐	☐	☐	☐	☐	☐
Check other equipment (if used)	☐	☐	☐	☐	☐	☐	☐
Look for odd behavior & signs of illness or fin damage.	☐	☐	☐	☐	☐	☐	☐

NOTES:

WEEKLY, MONTHLY CHECKLIST

- [ ] Test check water quality once a week
- [ ] Change 1/3 water 2 x week
- [ ] Vacuum up uneaten food and waste.
- [ ] Check pH and bacteria levels.

MONTHLY ACTIVITY   MONTH:

- [ ] Check filters, replacing media as necessary
- [ ] Clean fake plants, decorations, & algae
- [ ] Vacuum up all waste & uneaten food from gravel
- [ ] Check water quality & pH levels

HEALTH CHECKLIST   DATE:

- [Y] [N] Active and alert
- [Y] [N] Eats regularly
- [Y] [N] Vibrant colors
- [Y] [N] Undamaged fins
- [Y] [N] Reacts aggressively to outside stimulus

NOTES:

DAILY CHECKLIST

📅 Activity	WEEK OF						
	SUN	MON	TUE	WED	THU	FRI	SAT
Feed 2-4 pellets, 1 to 2 times daily.	☐	☐	☐	☐	☐	☐	☐
Remove uneaten food	☐	☐	☐	☐	☐	☐	☐
Check filter	☐	☐	☐	☐	☐	☐	☐
Check water temperature	☐	☐	☐	☐	☐	☐	☐
Check other equipment (if used)	☐	☐	☐	☐	☐	☐	☐
Look for odd behavior & signs of illness or fin damage.	☐	☐	☐	☐	☐	☐	☐

NOTES:

WEEKLY, MONTHLY CHECKLIST

WEEKLY ACTIVITY   DATE:

- [ ] Test check water quality once a week
- [ ] Change 1/3 water 2 x week
- [ ] Vacuum up uneaten food and waste.
- [ ] Check pH and bacteria levels.

MONTHLY ACTIVITY   MONTH:

- [ ] Check filters, replacing media as necessary
- [ ] Clean fake plants, decorations, & algae
- [ ] Vacuum up all waste & uneaten food from gravel
- [ ] Check water quality & pH levels

HEALTH CHECKLIST   DATE:

- Y N Active and alert
- Y N Eats regularly
- Y N Vibrant colors
- Y N Undamaged fins
- Y N Reacts aggressively to outside stimulus

NOTES:

DAILY CHECKLIST

Activity	WEEK OF
	SUN MON TUE WED THU FRI SAT

	Feed 2-4 pellets, 1 to 2 times daily.	☐ ☐ ☐ ☐ ☐ ☐ ☐
	Remove uneaten food	☐ ☐ ☐ ☐ ☐ ☐ ☐
	Check filter	☐ ☐ ☐ ☐ ☐ ☐ ☐
	Check water temperature	☐ ☐ ☐ ☐ ☐ ☐ ☐
	Check other equipment (if used)	☐ ☐ ☐ ☐ ☐ ☐ ☐
	Look for odd behavior & signs of illness or fin damage.	☐ ☐ ☐ ☐ ☐ ☐ ☐

NOTES:

WEEKLY, MONTHLY CHECKLIST

WEEKLY ACTIVITY   DATE: [   ]

- ☐ Test check water quality once a week
- ☐ Change 1/3 water 2 x week
- ☐ Vacuum up uneaten food and waste.
- ☐ Check pH and bacteria levels.

MONTHLY ACTIVITY   MONTH:

- ☐ Check filters, replacing media as necessary
- ☐ Clean fake plants, decorations, & algae
- ☐ Vacuum up all waste & uneaten food from gravel
- ☐ Check water quality & pH levels

HEALTH CHECKLIST   DATE: [   ]

- ☐ Y ☐ N Active and alert
- ☐ Y ☐ N Eats regularly
- ☐ Y ☐ N Vibrant colors
- ☐ Y ☐ N Undamaged fins
- ☐ Y ☐ N Reacts aggressively to outside stimulus

NOTES:

DAILY CHECKLIST

Activity	WEEK OF						
	SUN	MON	TUE	WED	THU	FRI	SAT
Feed 2-4 pellets, 1 to 2 times daily.	☐	☐	☐	☐	☐	☐	☐
Remove uneaten food	☐	☐	☐	☐	☐	☐	☐
Check filter	☐	☐	☐	☐	☐	☐	☐
Check water temperature	☐	☐	☐	☐	☐	☐	☐
Check other equipment (if used)	☐	☐	☐	☐	☐	☐	☐
Look for odd behavior & signs of illness or fin damage.	☐	☐	☐	☐	☐	☐	☐

NOTES:

WEEKLY, MONTHLY CHECKLIST

WEEKLY ACTIVITY   DATE:

- [ ] Test check water quality once a week
- [ ] Change 1/3 water 2 x week
- [ ] Vacuum up uneaten food and waste.
- [ ] Check pH and bacteria levels.

MONTHLY ACTIVITY   MONTH:

- [ ] Check filters, replacing media as necessary
- [ ] Clean fake plants, decorations, & algae
- [ ] Vacuum up all waste & uneaten food from gravel
- [ ] Check water quality & pH levels

HEALTH CHECKLIST   DATE:

- Y N Active and alert
- Y N Eats regularly
- Y N Vibrant colors
- Y N Undamaged fins
- Y N Reacts aggressively to outside stimulus

NOTES:

DAILY CHECKLIST

Activity	WEEK OF	SUN	MON	TUE	WED	THU	FRI	SAT
Feed 2-4 pellets, 1 to 2 times daily.		☐	☐	☐	☐	☐	☐	☐
Remove uneaten food		☐	☐	☐	☐	☐	☐	☐
Check filter		☐	☐	☐	☐	☐	☐	☐
Check water temperature		☐	☐	☐	☐	☐	☐	☐
Check other equipment (if used)		☐	☐	☐	☐	☐	☐	☐
Look for odd behavior & signs of illness or fin damage.		☐	☐	☐	☐	☐	☐	☐

NOTES:

WEEKLY, MONTHLY CHECKLIST

WEEKLY ACTIVITY   DATE: [   ]

- ☐ Test check water quality once a week
- ☐ Change 1/3 water 2 x week
- ☐ Vacuum up uneaten food and waste.
- ☐ Check pH and bacteria levels.

MONTHLY ACTIVITY   MONTH:

- ☐ Check filters, replacing media as necessary
- ☐ Clean fake plants, decorations, & algae
- ☐ Vacuum up all waste & uneaten food from gravel
- ☐ Check water quality & pH levels

HEALTH CHECKLIST   DATE: [   ]

- ☐Y ☐N Active and alert
- ☐Y ☐N Eats regularly
- ☐Y ☐N Vibrant colors
- ☐Y ☐N Undamaged fins
- ☐Y ☐N Reacts aggressively to outside stimulus

NOTES:

DAILY CHECKLIST

Activity	WEEK OF
	SUN MON TUE WED THU FRI SAT

Feed 2-4 pellets, 1 to 2 times daily. ☐ ☐ ☐ ☐ ☐ ☐ ☐

Remove uneaten food ☐ ☐ ☐ ☐ ☐ ☐ ☐

Check filter ☐ ☐ ☐ ☐ ☐ ☐ ☐

Check water temperature ☐ ☐ ☐ ☐ ☐ ☐ ☐

Check other equipment (if used) ☐ ☐ ☐ ☐ ☐ ☐ ☐

Look for odd behavior & signs of illness or fin damage. ☐ ☐ ☐ ☐ ☐ ☐ ☐

NOTES:

WEEKLY, MONTHLY CHECKLIST

WEEKLY ACTIVITY   DATE:

- ☐ Test check water quality once a week
- ☐ Change 1/3 water 2 x week
- ☐ Vacuum up uneaten food and waste.
- ☐ Check pH and bacteria levels.

MONTHLY ACTIVITY   MONTH:

- ☐ Check filters, replacing media as necessary
- ☐ Clean fake plants, decorations, & algae
- ☐ Vacuum up all waste & uneaten food from gravel
- ☐ Check water quality & pH levels

HEALTH CHECKLIST   DATE:

- ☐ Y ☐ N   Active and alert
- ☐ Y ☐ N   Eats regularly
- ☐ Y ☐ N   Vibrant colors
- ☐ Y ☐ N   Undamaged fins
- ☐ Y ☐ N   Reacts aggressively to outside stimulus

NOTES:

DAILY CHECKLIST

Activity	WEEK OF						
	SUN	MON	TUE	WED	THU	FRI	SAT
Feed 2-4 pellets, 1 to 2 times daily.	☐	☐	☐	☐	☐	☐	☐
Remove uneaten food	☐	☐	☐	☐	☐	☐	☐
Check filter	☐	☐	☐	☐	☐	☐	☐
Check water temperature	☐	☐	☐	☐	☐	☐	☐
Check other equipment (if used)	☐	☐	☐	☐	☐	☐	☐
Look for odd behavior & signs of illness or fin damage.	☐	☐	☐	☐	☐	☐	☐

NOTES:

WEEKLY, MONTHLY CHECKLIST

WEEKLY ACTIVITY   DATE:

- [ ] Test check water quality once a week
- [ ] Change 1/3 water 2 x week
- [ ] Vacuum up uneaten food and waste.
- [ ] Check pH and bacteria levels.

MONTHLY ACTIVITY   MONTH:

- [ ] Check filters, replacing media as necessary
- [ ] Clean fake plants, decorations, & algae
- [ ] Vacuum up all waste & uneaten food from gravel
- [ ] Check water quality & pH levels

HEALTH CHECKLIST   DATE:

- [Y] [N] Active and alert
- [Y] [N] Eats regularly
- [Y] [N] Vibrant colors
- [Y] [N] Undamaged fins
- [Y] [N] Reacts aggressively to outside stimulus

NOTES:

DAILY CHECKLIST

Activity	WEEK OF						
	SUN	MON	TUE	WED	THU	FRI	SAT
Feed 2-4 pellets, 1 to 2 times daily.	☐	☐	☐	☐	☐	☐	☐
Remove uneaten food	☐	☐	☐	☐	☐	☐	☐
Check filter	☐	☐	☐	☐	☐	☐	☐
Check water temperature	☐	☐	☐	☐	☐	☐	☐
Check other equipment (if used)	☐	☐	☐	☐	☐	☐	☐
Look for odd behavior & signs of illness or fin damage.	☐	☐	☐	☐	☐	☐	☐

NOTES:

WEEKLY, MONTHLY CHECKLIST

WEEKLY ACTIVITY   DATE: ☐

- ☐ Test check water quality once a week
- ☐ Change 1/3 water 2 x week
- ☐ Vacuum up uneaten food and waste.
- ☐ Check pH and bacteria levels.

MONTHLY ACTIVITY   MONTH: ☐

- ☐ Check filters, replacing media as necessary
- ☐ Clean fake plants, decorations, & algae
- ☐ Vacuum up all waste & uneaten food from gravel
- ☐ Check water quality & pH levels

HEALTH CHECKLIST   DATE: ☐

- Y ☐ N ☐ Active and alert
- Y ☐ N ☐ Eats regularly
- Y ☐ N ☐ Vibrant colors
- Y ☐ N ☐ Undamaged fins
- Y ☐ N ☐ Reacts aggressively to outside stimulus

NOTES:

DAILY CHECKLIST

Activity	WEEK OF						
	SUN	MON	TUE	WED	THU	FRI	SAT
Feed 2-4 pellets, 1 to 2 times daily.	☐	☐	☐	☐	☐	☐	☐
Remove uneaten food	☐	☐	☐	☐	☐	☐	☐
Check filter	☐	☐	☐	☐	☐	☐	☐
Check water temperature	☐	☐	☐	☐	☐	☐	☐
Check other equipment (if used)	☐	☐	☐	☐	☐	☐	☐
Look for odd behavior & signs of illness or fin damage.	☐	☐	☐	☐	☐	☐	☐

NOTES:

WEEKLY, MONTHLY CHECKLIST

WEEKLY ACTIVITY   DATE: [   ]

- [ ] Test check water quality once a week
- [ ] Change 1/3 water 2 x week
- [ ] Vacuum up uneaten food and waste.
- [ ] Check pH and bacteria levels.

MONTHLY ACTIVITY   MONTH:

- [ ] Check filters, replacing media as necessary
- [ ] Clean fake plants, decorations, & algae
- [ ] Vacuum up all waste & uneaten food from gravel
- [ ] Check water quality & pH levels

HEALTH CHECKLIST   DATE: [   ]

- [Y] [N] Active and alert
- [Y] [N] Eats regularly
- [Y] [N] Vibrant colors
- [Y] [N] Undamaged fins
- [Y] [N] Reacts aggressively to outside stimulus

NOTES:

DAILY CHECKLIST

Activity	WEEK OF						
	SUN	MON	TUE	WED	THU	FRI	SAT
Feed 2-4 pellets, 1 to 2 times daily.	☐	☐	☐	☐	☐	☐	☐
Remove uneaten food	☐	☐	☐	☐	☐	☐	☐
Check filter	☐	☐	☐	☐	☐	☐	☐
Check water temperature	☐	☐	☐	☐	☐	☐	☐
Check other equipment (if used)	☐	☐	☐	☐	☐	☐	☐
Look for odd behavior & signs of illness or fin damage.	☐	☐	☐	☐	☐	☐	☐

NOTES:

WEEKLY, MONTHLY CHECKLIST

- [ ] Test check water quality once a week
- [ ] Change 1/3 water 2 x week
- [ ] Vacuum up uneaten food and waste.
- [ ] Check pH and bacteria levels.

MONTHLY ACTIVITY   MONTH:

- [ ] Check filters, replacing media as necessary
- [ ] Clean fake plants, decorations, & algae
- [ ] Vacuum up all waste & uneaten food from gravel
- [ ] Check water quality & pH levels

HEALTH CHECKLIST   DATE:

- [Y] [N] Active and alert
- [Y] [N] Eats regularly
- [Y] [N] Vibrant colors
- [Y] [N] Undamaged fins
- [Y] [N] Reacts aggressively to outside stimulus

NOTES:

DAILY CHECKLIST

Activity	WEEK OF						
	SUN	MON	TUE	WED	THU	FRI	SAT
Feed 2-4 pellets, 1 to 2 times daily.	☐	☐	☐	☐	☐	☐	☐
Remove uneaten food	☐	☐	☐	☐	☐	☐	☐
Check filter	☐	☐	☐	☐	☐	☐	☐
Check water temperature	☐	☐	☐	☐	☐	☐	☐
Check other equipment (if used)	☐	☐	☐	☐	☐	☐	☐
Look for odd behavior & signs of illness or fin damage.	☐	☐	☐	☐	☐	☐	☐

NOTES:

WEEKLY, MONTHLY CHECKLIST

WEEKLY ACTIVITY   DATE:

- [ ] Test check water quality once a week
- [ ] Change 1/3 water 2 x week
- [ ] Vacuum up uneaten food and waste.
- [ ] Check pH and bacteria levels.

MONTHLY ACTIVITY   MONTH:

- [ ] Check filters, replacing media as necessary
- [ ] Clean fake plants, decorations, & algae
- [ ] Vacuum up all waste & uneaten food from gravel
- [ ] Check water quality & pH levels

HEALTH CHECKLIST   DATE:

- [Y] [N] Active and alert
- [Y] [N] Eats regularly
- [Y] [N] Vibrant colors
- [Y] [N] Undamaged fins
- [Y] [N] Reacts aggressively to outside stimulus

NOTES:

DAILY CHECKLIST

Activity	WEEK OF						
	SUN	MON	TUE	WED	THU	FRI	SAT
Feed 2-4 pellets, 1 to 2 times daily.	☐	☐	☐	☐	☐	☐	☐
Remove uneaten food	☐	☐	☐	☐	☐	☐	☐
Check filter	☐	☐	☐	☐	☐	☐	☐
Check water temperature	☐	☐	☐	☐	☐	☐	☐
Check other equipment (if used)	☐	☐	☐	☐	☐	☐	☐
Look for odd behavior & signs of illness or fin damage.	☐	☐	☐	☐	☐	☐	☐

NOTES:

WEEKLY, MONTHLY CHECKLIST

- [ ] Test check water quality once a week
- [ ] Change 1/3 water 2 x week
- [ ] Vacuum up uneaten food and waste.
- [ ] Check pH and bacteria levels.

MONTHLY ACTIVITY   MONTH:

- [ ] Check filters, replacing media as necessary
- [ ] Clean fake plants, decorations, & algae
- [ ] Vacuum up all waste & uneaten food from gravel
- [ ] Check water quality & pH levels

HEALTH CHECKLIST   DATE:

- [Y] [N] Active and alert
- [Y] [N] Eats regularly
- [Y] [N] Vibrant colors
- [Y] [N] Undamaged fins
- [Y] [N] Reacts aggressively to outside stimulus

NOTES:

MY PET
BETTA FISH LOGBOOK

Made in the USA
Las Vegas, NV
07 February 2024

85420694R00069